of FOOD

Peter Bringe

© 2012 by Peter Bringe
All rights reserved.
ISBN: 978-0-615-58944-2
Printed in the United States of America

If you would like to contact the author,
please e-mail him at peterjb@truevine.net

Scripture quotations are from
The Holy Bible, English Standard Version,
copyright © 2001 by Crossway Bibles,
a division of Good News Publishers.
Used by permission. All rights reserved.

Editing by Josiah Hamill
Typesetting by Anna Storrie
Cover design by Ray Suzuki

To my father who has taught me so much about many things, especially about the glory of God as seen in His creation. Without his teaching around the dinner table on God's glorious provision of good food, this book would definitely not have happened.

To my mother who has lovingly cared for me and has also implemented my father's love for God's creation by making beautiful and nutritious food day after day (even when I did not want it), and for teaching me a love of hospitality and fellowship around the dinner table.

To my fathers and mothers of previous generations who have given me a godly heritage and a good work ethic, to my grandfather who worked hard in agriculture as an extension agent, and to the generations of my ancestors who have worked as farmers throughout history.

To my heavenly Father, the Triune God, Creator and Sustainer of everything, Who has saved me from eternal judgment into a covenantal relationship with Him, and who has given me His Word as the guide for life. Anything that my family or I have done that is good or praiseworthy is only because of His grace, and to Him be all the glory.

Contents

Introduction to Food ~ 7

Food and Health ~ 13

Food and Culture ~ 27

Food and Economics ~ 43

Food and the Creation ~ 63

Conclusion ~ 73

One

INTRODUCTION TO FOOD

How then shall we eat? In recent times there has been an onslaught of diets, studies, research, claims, disputes, lawsuits, movies, and books all on the subject of food. There is much confusion about the subject of food, especially since the centralization of science and food is now in question, and everyone seems to be an expert with his own set of ideas about food. We are at a time like the Protestant Reformation of the 1500s when the centralized Roman Catholic Church was called into question, motivating the common man to study the Scripture for himself. This was a great opportunity for Christians to go back to Scripture and build from a solid foundation. On the other hand it also allowed the Anabaptists and other unorthodox and autonomous sects to form and overreact. Nowadays, the centralized food industry is called into question, so the common man is now researching food for himself. This is great because it allows us to get back to what Scripture says on the subject and build on it, but it also allows for many independent overreactions that become the Anabaptists of the food industry.

I have grown up in a unique environment. First of all, I am used to decentralization because my parents discipled my siblings and me at home rather than sending us to the public schools. This allowed me to get "unplugged" from the centralized government system of education, enabling me to study God's world from a Biblical perspective. Secondly, my father, Neal Bringe, is a Ph.D. food scientist who has worked in the food industry since 1989. Our dinnertime discussions have oftentimes revolved around the nutrition and the beauty of food, both from a scientific and a cultural point of view. Over the years my father has imparted much wisdom to me through this relational discipleship on food. This knowledge gives me the credentials I use to write this book. I do not have a degree in food or nutrition, but I draw from the teachings of my father as well as from other godly men like my pastor. These men have formed my thinking and given me a balanced and unique perspective on the subject. By God's grace I hope that this book will help others to realize the great eternal truths found in God's Word that will help us to rebuild a proper understanding of food during the great confusion of our day.

What is so important about food? Is it really worth this much attention? On a basic level we can see that though we make our food, our food also makes us. You cannot escape food. It is one of the basic needs to survive; there are few others that are more integrated into our lives. What else have you done three times a day for your entire life? What we choose to eat affects our life tremendously, and our life affects what food we choose. It is vitally important to think about our food. In this book we will be going through its interactions with our lives as we study this gift from the Lord God Almighty.

Food is a sensitive subject for people because it is so ingrained into who they are. Food not only sustains us physically, but it also feeds a part of our emotional needs as well. Food is a way to celebrate and a way to mourn. It is a way to remember and a way to look forward. It is something we make decisions about constantly, and thus it reveals who we are. What we do is a result of who we are. What our beliefs are about things will determine how we interact with them. Food is part of our culture and view of life. It shows what we value and what we believe. For example, if one believes that pleasure has ultimate value, he will eat food that produces maximum sensual taste and pleasure. If one believes that his mortal life has ultimate value, he will either be dominated by taking good care of his body, or he will lose hope and not care what he eats. Ideas have consequences, and what people eat illustrates this principle.

Food is studied by nutritionists and chefs alike. Generally speaking, the scientific nutritionist looks at food as being composed of both healthful nutrients and harmful toxins or bacteria, mostly disregarding the art of food. Then the chefs look at the taste and presentation of food with little regard for health consequences. You either end up with food that is nutritious but tasteless or very tasty food that is a "heart-attack on a plate." Thus, food is a complex subject because it is a source of both nutrition and beauty. Both are important to Christians. As Christians, our whole persons are valuable, both the soul and the body, and thus health is important and not to be set aside as something that only "health nuts" think about. "I appeal to you therefore, brothers, by the mercies of God, to present your bodies as a living sacrifice, holy and acceptable to God" (Rom. 12:1). "If you have found honey, eat only enough for you, lest you have your fill of it and vomit it" (Prov. 25:16). But the beauty of it—the look, the smell, the taste, the surrounding atmosphere and emotions—is also important. "My son, eat honey, for it is good, and the drippings of the honeycomb are sweet to your taste" (Prov. 24:13). It is the balance between the scientific journal, which is full of information that is mostly dry and impractical, and the novel, which is full of feelings that might be foolish. So we must balance food that is healthy with food that brings the right emotions for the occasion. We will see what the Bible says on these values in food, and we will also find that these aspects are not necessarily opposed to each other but are interconnected and can work together.

How we eat is just as important as what we eat. Much of our culture is built around materialism where work is merely a means to gain material wealth. To work for anything that does not produce goods is seen as extra and unnecessary work. This includes music, dance, painting, religion, family, non-business relationships, quality food, etc. Many meals are eaten on the way to the next meeting or event in order to keep us going. People want quick meals that they can get out of the way so they can get back to business. Food is not seen as something worth working for in a kitchen (unless your paycheck happens to come by doing so). Our food then

INTRODUCTION TO FOOD

loses quality and merely defaults to a contest to produce the cheapest, most convenient, and most sensuously pleasing edible stuff that inevitably has a few milligrams of the latest scientifically-studied chemical to ease the guilty conscience. As we will see, this is not the Biblical view of work or of food.

Food is part of God's creation, and our view of creation will affect how we look at food. If one is prideful and disregards God's design, he will rely on his own human powers to process food into a new creation. When man in his pride tries to revolt against the Creator and make his own world, he can't help corrupting it because mankind is depraved and sinful (Rom. 3:12). One may also err if he worships the creation instead of the Creator. He then will become content to let the world be and become the "noble savage" that humanists love. He forgets that we are called to take dominion of the world and work to make it fruitful. "The Lord God took the man and put him in the garden of Eden to work it and keep it" (Gen. 2:15). "Be fruitful and multiply and fill the earth and subdue it, and have dominion over the fish of the sea and over the birds of the heavens and over every living thing that moves on the earth" (Gen. 1:28). We will look at food as a part of God's creation and examine how we are to view and use it.

Thus we enter the subject of the Christian view of food. Is it a tool for survival? Is it an expression of personality and emotions? Is it a part of what a beautiful home environment should be? Is it an amazing creation by God that we are to carefully use? Is it all of the above?

Two

FOOD AND HEALTH

"The fear of the Lord is the beginning of knowledge; fools despise wisdom and instruction."

—Proverbs 1:7

The basis for knowledge and wisdom is the fear of the Lord. Without the fear of the Lord, our thinking will be based upon faulty reasoning, so we will not know things correctly. The Word of God is the only source of absolute truth because it is the Word of the perfectly truthful God. Everything else is tainted by sin. Only when we are humble before God can we come to the knowledge of the truth and the wisdom to use that knowledge to discern right from wrong and blessing from curse. Only then can our observations be interpreted correctly. Only then can we know what is good. This realization is important to any discussion of health. Proverbs specifically says:

> "Be not wise in your own eyes; fear the Lord, and turn away from evil. It will be *healing to your flesh* and *refreshment to your bones.*"
>
> —Proverbs 3:7–8, emphasis added

The Christian Philosophy of Food

So when figuring out which foods are most (or least) beneficial, let us humbly submit ourselves to the only standard of absolute truth—the Bible.

> "Or do you not know that your body is a temple of the Holy Spirit within you, whom you have from God? You are not your own, for you were bought with a price. So glorify God in your body."
> —1 Corinthians 6:19–20

We see from the above verse that our physical bodies are important. The Bible does not teach Gnosticism (where the spiritual is good and valuable, and the physical is evil and dispensable). Instead the Bible teaches us to take dominion of the earth and to pray, "Your kingdom come...on earth as it is in heaven" (Matt. 6:10). It teaches us that whole Christians are redeemed, including their bodies, and will be resurrected to eternal life (Rom. 8:11). It teaches us that Christian bodies are temples of the Holy Spirit, and that these temples are God's (1 Cor. 6:19–20). The spiritual and the physical affect each other; our soul affects our bodily condition, and vice versa. As missionary Amy Carmichael is said to have replied to accusations of caring too much for physical needs, "Souls are more or less firmly attached to bodies." When we love the Lord, we act in physical actions on this earth for His glory, and so, out of the desire to do God's work, we should keep our bodies functioning properly. We should glorify God in the way that we treat "our" bodies.

People today are familiar with food pyramids, where the foods primarily eaten are on the bottom, and those that are sparingly eaten are on top. The Bible presents a very simple food pyramid that is progressively revealed in Scripture.

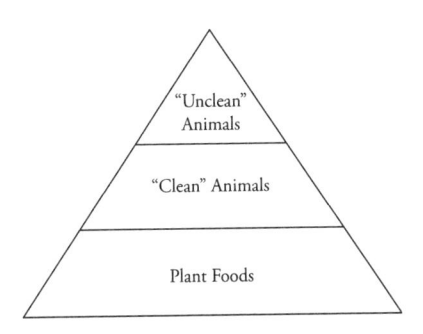

```
        /\
       /  \
      /"Unclean"\
     / Animals  \
    /------------\
   / "Clean" Animals \
  /--------------------\
 /     Plant Foods      \
/_____\
```

Plant Foods

In the beginning God gave Adam and Eve plants to eat.

> "And God said, 'Behold, I have given you every plant yielding seed that is on the face of all the earth, and every tree with seed in its fruit. You shall have them for food.'"
> —Genesis 1:29

Only plants were made as food in the beginning, for animals as well as for man. Even after the Fall, mankind was restricted to only eating plant foods until after the flood. It would follow that plant foods are the foundational food for mankind. It is as if you have a computer program and get an update for the program. The program is basic, while the update is an extra bonus that might be very good with the program but does not work by itself. Some people have a very negative response to the mentioning of plant foods and want to avoid any connection with the "dreaded" vegetarians. To put your mind at ease, I am not saying that the Bible commands us to eat plant foods only. However, I am saying that the Bible teaches that plants are more central and important. This principle is not out of place in the rest of Scripture. For example, in the 40 years in the wilderness, God gave the Israelites manna (a bread-like substance) and quail. Manna was the more basic food, and the Israelites were punished with a plague for their selfish craving of meat (Num. 11:32–34). In Proverbs 23:20 the Bible also warns against being among the "gluttonous eaters of meat." Daniel groups meat with wine as delicacies that he refrained from while mourning (Dan. 10:3). It seems that our modern culture with its meat-centric meals is out of line with a Biblical view of meat.

Some will object that you need meat to get enough protein to build muscle. However, plants, especially vegetables, legumes, and nuts, have more protein than people realize, and the protein they do have comes with less calories and more nutrients unique to plants. For example, broccoli contains more protein per calorie than steak. About half of the dry weight of spinach is protein. Try looking at the apes and gorillas and say that meat is necessary to build muscle. Perhaps the mother that told you to eat your broccoli was right.

A predominately plant food diet is a defense against the argument that we cannot produce enough food for a growing population and so should not obey God's command to "Be fruitful and multiply and fill the earth" (Gen. 1:28). Plant foods are a more efficient source of food in most regions. Because Western nations and those that they influence (like modern China) primarily eat meat with plants on the side, agriculture is not up to its potential production. An acre of land used for cattle can supply one adult's protein needs for 77 days, but if it is used for soybeans, it can supply an adult's protein needs for 2,224 days.[1] In one study it is calculated that "land use for fruit and dry bean production is...~5 and ~3 times, respectively, more efficient than land use for animal production."[2] When driving across places like Illinois or Iowa where the sea of corn and soybeans seems to be unending, it brings up the question, "Where does this all go?" A large percentage goes to animal feed. We then eat the animals and receive only a fraction of the nutrients that the plants could have provided. If we cut back the field corn, soybeans, and water for animals and instead grew sweet corn and other vegetables for food, we would increase the food and water supply by a huge amount. By eating more plant foods, we are taking better and more efficient dominion of the earth.

Meat

Even though plant foods are more basic to our diets, God has also given us meat to eat:

"Every moving thing that lives shall be food for you. And as I gave you the green plants, I give you

---

[1] Jethro Kloss, *Back to Eden,* (Loma Linda, CA: Back to Eden Books Publishing, 1992), 601.

[2] Gidon Eshel & Pamela A Martin, "Geophysics and nutritional science: toward a novel, unified paradigm," *The American Journal of Clinical Nutrition* 89 (suppl) (2009): 1714S.

everything. But you shall not eat flesh with its life, that is, its blood. And for your lifeblood I will require a reckoning: from every beast I will require it and from man. From his fellow man I will require a reckoning for the life of man.
'Whoever sheds the blood of man,
by man shall his blood be shed,
for God made man in his own image.'"
—Genesis 9:3–6

The first thing that is apparent is the importance of not eating the blood. Some people explain this as a ceremonial law which was fulfilled in Christ. But if this is ceremonial, then why does God in the same breath proclaim the sanctity of life and capital punishment as the foundations of civil government? Are those ceremonial as well? I think not. When you look at this Bible passage closer, you will realize that this command is given to Noah, and it thus precedes Abraham, Moses, and the ceremonial laws of Israel. Even in the New Testament, the council of Jerusalem came to agree that,

> "It has seemed good to the Holy Spirit and to us to lay on you no greater burden than these requirements: that you abstain from what has been sacrificed to idols, and from blood, and from what has been strangled, and from sexual immorality. If you keep yourselves from these, you will do well. Farewell."
> —Acts 15:28–29

As Christians, even though we kill animals and eat them, we still value life and do not drink blood like pagans.

It is interesting to note that after the Flood every living thing that moves was given as food (Gen. 9:3), even though there was already a distinction between clean and unclean animals when it came to sacrifices.

> "Then Noah built an altar to the Lord and took some of every clean animal and some of every clean bird and offered burnt offerings on the altar."
> —Genesis 8:20

This was to change with the distinction of unclean and clean animals made in the Law given to Moses.

"Clean" Animals

"And the Lord spoke to Moses and Aaron, saying to them, 'Speak to the people of Israel, saying, These are the living things that you may eat among all the animals that are on the earth. Whatever parts the hoof and is cloven-footed and chews the cud, among the animals, you may eat....

"'These you may eat, of all that are in the waters. Everything in the waters that has fins and scales, whether in the seas or in the rivers, you may eat. But anything in the seas or the rivers that has not fins and scales, of the swarming creatures in the waters and of the living creatures that are in the waters, is detestable to you....

"'And these you shall detest among the birds; they shall not be eaten; they are detestable: the eagle, the

The Christian Philosophy of Food

bearded vulture, the black vulture, the kite, the falcon of any kind, every raven of any kind, the ostrich, the nighthawk, the sea gull, the hawk of any kind, the little owl, the cormorant, the short-eared owl, the barn owl, the tawny owl, the carrion vulture, the stork, the heron of any kind, the hoopoe, and the bat.

"'All winged insects that go on all fours are detestable to you. Yet among the winged insects that go on all fours you may eat those that have jointed legs above their feet, with which to hop on the ground....

"'Every animal that parts the hoof but is not cloven-footed or does not chew the cud is unclean to you. Everyone who touches them shall be unclean. And all that walk on their paws, among the animals that go on all fours, are unclean to you. Whoever touches their carcass shall be unclean until the evening....

"'And these are unclean to you among the swarming things that swarm on the ground: the mole rat, the mouse, the great lizard of any kind, the gecko, the monitor lizard, the lizard, the sand lizard, and the chameleon. These are unclean to you among all that swarm. Whoever touches them when they are dead shall be unclean until the evening....

"'Whatever goes on its belly, and whatever goes on all fours, or whatever has many feet, any swarming thing that swarms on the ground, you shall not eat, for they are detestable....

"'For I am the Lord your God. Consecrate yourselves therefore, and be holy, for I am holy. You shall not defile yourselves with any swarming thing that crawls on the ground. For I am the Lord who brought you up out of the land of Egypt to be your God. You shall therefore be holy, for I am holy.'"
—Leviticus 11:1–3, 9–10, 13–21, 26–27, 29–31, 42, 44–45

Before we quickly dismiss the applicability of this law to us, let us remember that all Scripture is profitable (2 Tim. 3:16). We will get to where Jesus declares all foods clean, but let us first look at God's main instructions about food.

God in His wisdom as the Creator of the world set apart some animals from the rest as food. For the most part it is pretty obvious which animals are meant for food and which are not. Among the unclean animals we find predators, scavengers, and filters, such as bears, vultures, and mussels. They have less efficient digestive systems and will collect more toxins in their bodies from the animals they eat (some, like shellfish, are designed to clean the environment by hoarding chemicals and toxins). The clean animals are more often herbivores, have better physiological systems to remove toxins, and are more commonly eaten by other animals. There are few studies comparing clean and unclean foods, but those studies point to the wisdom of God's instruction. The most thorough research was done in 1953 by Dr. David Macht of Johns Hopkins University that reported on the toxic effects of animal flesh. Without exception, all the clean animals that were studied were classified as non-toxic while all the unclean animals were classified as toxic.[3] While we might not always understand why certain animals are unclean, we should have faith in God's Word and take seriously His directions on what we should eat.

"Unclean" Animals

"'There is nothing outside a person that by going into him can defile him, but the things that come out of a person are what defile him.' And when he had entered the house and left the people, his disciples asked him about the parable. And he said to them, 'Then are you also without understanding? Do you not see that whatever goes into a person from outside cannot defile him, since it enters not his heart but his stomach, and is expelled?' (Thus he declared all foods clean.)"
—Mark 7:15–19

"In it were all kinds of animals and reptiles and birds of the air. And there came a voice to him: 'Rise, Peter; kill and eat.' But Peter said, 'By no means, Lord; for I have never eaten anything that is common or unclean.' And the voice came to him again a second time, 'What God has made clean, do not call common.'

---

[3] Rex Russell, M.D., *What the Bible Says about Healthy Living* (Grand Rapids, MI: Fleming H. Revell, 1999), 76.

This happened three times, and the thing was taken up at once to heaven."
—Acts 10:12–16

And finally, the third food group is the unclean (or formerly unclean) foods. The main purpose of the clean and unclean regulations was holiness and the avoidance of defilement (Lev. 11:44–45). These were to set apart the people of the Holy God as a righteous and pure people. While we have already been made holy (set apart for righteousness) by the blood of Christ, we are also being sanctified (being made holy) by the Holy Spirit. In Mark 7:15–19 (above) Jesus shows the importance of being holy and undefiled in our heart. Our external works are only important as much as they are the outworking of an internal faith. It is in this context that Jesus declares all foods clean. Eating unclean foods no longer spiritually defiles us, but evil thoughts do (as always). As the next three verses say,

> "For from within, out of the heart of man, come evil thoughts, sexual immorality, theft, murder, adultery, coveting, wickedness, deceit, sensuality, envy, slander, pride, foolishness. All these evil things come from within, and they defile a person."
> —Mark 7:21–23

Notice that from within come murder (i.e. disregard of life), sensuality, pride, and foolishness, which can all lead to unhealthy eating. Just because all foods are clean doesn't mean that we can eat whatever we want. As New Testament Christians we have been given a greater outpouring of the

Holy Spirit and thus have increased maturity. Instead of needing very specific laws regarding every possible situation, we should be able to apply God's laws to our situations with wisdom. We are still to eat wisely, and the old clean and unclean distinctions are still helpful. But it is our attitude in the way we eat that can defile us, not specific foods.

We ought to rejoice that God has given us such a variety of food to eat. This expansion of food choices to "Every moving thing that lives" (Gen. 9:3) benefits us in various ways. It helps us to take dominion over the earth. If you were going exploring in the Amazon, you would be glad to know that, if you had to, you could eat snails and worms. As Acts 10 illustrates, it signifies the expansion of the gospel to all peoples and cultures. Therefore, when you go to your neighbors' house, and they serve you pork, you can eat it rather than offend your host. It helps us remember that though food is important, it is not the substance of our faith.

> "For the kingdom of God is not a matter of eating and drinking but of righteousness and peace and joy in the Holy Spirit."
>
> —Romans 14:17

But remember, as John Calvin states, "Liberty is one thing—the use of it is another."[4]

When we listen to what God has told us and follow His directions, they are a blessing! In ancient Rome the pagans

---

4 John Calvin, "Commentary on Corinthians," http://www.ccel.org/ccel/calvin/calcom39.xiii.iii.html (accessed December 2, 2011).

were jealous of the protection that the early Christians and Jews had against epidemics. In the Middle Ages, when the black plague swept through Europe, the Jews were much less affected by it because they still followed God's instructions on food and cleanliness.[5] If we have the faith to obey God, we will be blessed by Him. God is good, and His guidance in life by His law is a blessing. God has said in Exodus 15:26,

> "If you will diligently listen to the voice of the Lord your God, and do that which is right in his eyes, and give ear to his commandments and keep all his statutes, I will put none of the diseases on you that I put on the Egyptians, for I am the Lord, your healer."

While there will be other observations in this book that concern health (such as relates to self-control or our view of creation), the basic instructions we have from the Bible on what we should eat are the following:

1. As God's holy people we should be healthy and clean, and we should take care of our redeemed bodies.

2. Our primary foods should be plant-based since they were given as food in the beginning.

3. Though we are given animals to eat, we show respect for life by not drinking the blood.

4. Our primary animal foods should be those "clean" animals specified by God.

---

[5] Russell, *What the Bible Says about Healthy Living*, 42.

5. We are given "every moving thing that lives" (Gen. 9:3) as food, so we should rejoice in the freedom we have. However, we should remember, "'All things are lawful,' but not all things are helpful. 'All things are lawful,' but not all things build up" (1 Cor. 10:23).

Three

FOOD AND CULTURE

"For everything there is a season, and a time for every matter under heaven: a time to be born, and a time to die; a time to plant, and a time to pluck up what is planted; a time to kill, and a time to heal; a time to break down, and a time to build up; a time to weep, and a time to laugh; a time to mourn, and a time to dance; a time to cast away stones, and a time to gather stones together; a time to embrace, and a time to refrain from embracing; a time to seek, and a time to lose; a time to keep, and a time to cast away; a time to tear, and a time to sew; a time to keep silence, and a time to speak; a time to love, and a time to hate; a time for war, and a time for peace."
—Ecclesiastes 3:1–8

Is food merely for health? Not at all! There are many books on health out there that people think of as "food books," but in fact they only deal with scientific nutrition. Food is part of our culture. Our culture is expressive of what we think, feel, and do. It is very intertwined with our life. It deals with our emotions and personalities, our history and our situations.

The Christian Philosophy of Food

Our food means something. Our food is not isolated from its context. In this chapter I will present some Biblical examples of the way food is used in culture and life.

Food and Rejoicing

In the Bible (as well as throughout time), food is used to celebrate and rejoice. In Deuteronomy 16:15 we see God commanding Israel to keep the Feast of Booths and rejoice during the harvest time for God's provision of food:

> "For seven days you shall keep the feast to the Lord your God at the place that the Lord will choose, because the Lord your God will bless you in all your produce and in all the work of your hands, so that you will be altogether joyful."

We can see this principle applied in our own culture with the rural harvest festivals and our American holiday of Thanksgiving. What is a better way to rejoice in God's provision of our daily bread than to eat some of that bread? Whenever we eat there should be joy and thanksgiving in what God has provided for us to eat.

Food is also used in other celebrations, such as when the prodigal son returns home.

> "But the father said to his servants, 'Bring quickly the best robe, and put it on him, and put a ring on his hand, and shoes on his feet. And bring the fattened calf and kill it, and let us eat and celebrate. For this

my son was dead, and is alive again; he was lost, and is found.' And they began to celebrate."
—Luke 15:22–24 (for another example, see also Deuteronomy 14:22–29)

Again feasting and celebrating are intertwined. And this isn't any small supper; this is a feast with the fattened calf. There is a time to eat conservatively, paying close attention to health and such, but there are also times to feast and make merry. In fact, if you do not normally eat conservatively, celebrations lose their "specialness." For example, people today eat fattened calves almost every day, so to celebrate they need to get the "suicide on a plate" kind of meals that people of older cultures would have found disgusting. This principle is a rebuke to both those who are overly health-conscious and those who are overly indulgent. To those who are overly health conscious: it is sometimes fitting to eat some foods (like a fatted calf) that might not be as healthy as broccoli but will add to the rejoicing. And to those who are overly indulgent: if you normally eat like it's a celebration, what are you supposed to eat during a real celebration? The connection of food to celebration is also seen in the next example of food and mourning.

Food and Mourning

As food has been historically related with rejoicing, the abstaining from food has been synonymous with distress, repentance, and mourning. For example, when Mordecai and the Israelites heard the decree of the King for their destruction,

> "There was great mourning among the Jews, with fasting and weeping and lamenting, and many of them lay in sackcloth and ashes."
> —Esther 4:3

When Ezra and the Israelites were traveling to rebuild the Temple and were in danger of attacks, Ezra records that,

> "I proclaimed a fast there, at the river Ahava, that we might humble ourselves before our God, to seek from him a safe journey for ourselves, our children, and all our goods."
> —Ezra 8:21

Fasting has become somewhat of a lost art, largely because it has been frequently abused. When people use it as a way to merit God's favor, it becomes a man-centered superstition. But fasting can be good and beneficial. In his *Institutes of the Christian Religion,* John Calvin sums up the proper purposes of fasting in three categories: fasts to subdue and control the flesh, fasts to prepare for prayer and meditation, and fasts to give evidence of humility and guilt before God. He explains:

> "The first end is not very often regarded in public fasting, because all have not the same bodily constitution, nor the same state of health, and hence it is more applicable to private fasting. The second end is common to both, for this preparation for prayer is requisite for the whole Church, as well as for each individual member. The same thing may be said of the third. For it sometimes happens that God smites a nation with war or pestilence, or some kind

of calamity. In this common chastisement it behooves the whole people to plead guilty, and confess their guilt. Should the hand of the Lord strike any one in private, then the same thing is to be done by himself alone, or by his family. The thing, indeed, is properly a feeling of the mind. But when the mind is affected as it ought, it cannot but give vent to itself in external manifestation, especially when it tends to the common edification, that all, by openly confessing their sin, may render praise to the divine justice, and by their example mutually encourage each other."[1]

The first purpose of fasting does not have to do with mourning, but for its beneficial effects on the body.

First, our bodies need rest to digest the food they have eaten and to expel toxins from our cells. This is usually done when we fast from dinnertime in the evening until "breakfast" the next morning. But for some people this is not always enough, and it has been shown that partial or full fasting can help with many health problems.[2]

Second, fasting (whether with no food or limited food) can help the exercise of self-control over the impulses of the flesh. Self-control is a big part of health, and it is nothing less than a fruit of the Holy Spirit (Gal. 5:22–23) in those who belong to Christ and "have crucified the flesh with its passions and desires" (Gal. 5:24). Christians living by the power of the Spirit should not be captivated by snacks, but they instead

---

[1] John Calvin, *Institutes,* trans. Henry Beveridge (Peabody, MA: Hendrickson Publishers, Inc., 2008), 820.

[2] Russell, *What the Bible Says about Healthy Living,* 43–50.

should exercise self-control by holding their bodies in subjection. A selfish man-centered lifestyle leads to addiction and destruction. Paul describes the enemies of the cross of Christ thus: "Their end is destruction, their god is their belly" (Phil. 3:19). Even though a food might be good in itself, if it becomes an addiction, we should probably take complete control and abstain from it at least for a time. For example, though we are permitted to drink wine (Ps. 104:14–15; Prov. 3:9–10; John 2:1–11), and Timothy was even encouraged to (1 Tim. 5:23), the Bible also warns against being addicted to wine (Prov. 20:1, 23:29–35; Eph. 5:18; Titus 2:3). In some cases abstinence is approved or even commanded (Judg. 13:14; Prov. 31:4; Jer. 35). Even though wine might be a classic example, this principle also applies to any food. We ought to depend on God for peace and joy rather than on our food. We are to control our bodies and let them have the rest they need.

Calvin's third use is the one we are probably most familiar with. It is perhaps the easiest one to misuse as well, but, as Calvin points out, if we truly feel sorrowful and distressed, we will express ourselves in how we eat. It is a fact that when we are sad, we don't want to eat as much as usual, and eating may even cause us harm when we are stressed. When we fast, we give ourselves more time to focus on what we have done and cry out to God for forgiveness. When we fast, the reasons for our fasting are constantly prominent in our minds because our natural instincts will be continually asking, "Why?" Although we should not be prideful in our repentance, we should confess our sins to one another (James 5:16), as individuals especially, but also as families (Josh. 7:19–21), churches (Joel 1:14), and nations (Jon. 3:6–10).

> "Consecrate a fast; call a solemn assembly. Gather the elders and all the inhabitants of the land to the house of the Lord your God, and cry out to the Lord."
> —Joel 1:14

Food and Remembering

> "This day shall be for you a memorial day, and you shall keep it as a feast to the Lord; throughout your generations, as a statute forever, you shall keep it as a feast."
> —Exodus 12:14

History is a very important part of the Bible. Not only are many of the books historical narratives, but throughout Scripture we are commanded to remember what God has done in the past. When God gave the Ten Commandments, He called to attention the history of the Israelites by calling Himself the God "who brought you out of the land of Egypt, out of the house of slavery" (Deut. 5:6). When the people of Israel crossed over the Jordan, God commanded them to set up twelve stones as a "memorial forever" (Josh. 4:7). When the Ark was returned to Jerusalem, David rejoiced by singing: "Remember the wondrous works that he has done, his miracles and the judgments he uttered" (1 Chron. 16:12). David also proclaims, "I will remember the deeds of the Lord; yes, I will remember your wonders of old" (Ps. 77:11). It was when the people forgot what God had done, and what the consequences of their past sins were, that they fell into condemnation and judgment. To clarify, the deeds of the Lord include all of history (Deut. 2:20–33; Job 38; Matt. 10:29).

Something as important as history is not to be artificially separated from life by means of a classroom, but it is something to be integrated into our life. Our culture should have a historic awareness about it, and that includes our food. A great example of this is in the Old Testament feasts such as Passover.

> "Seven days you shall eat it with unleavened bread, the bread of affliction—for you came out of the land of Egypt in haste—that all the days of your life you may remember the day when you came out of the land of Egypt."
> –Deuteronomy 16:3

The works of God in history were integrated into the culture and food of the Israelites. When they ate the unleavened bread, they would think of God's deliverance from Egypt and would form a physical connection with God's salvation of His people.

We can see this remembering of history in traditional meals practiced today in various ways. For example, when Scots eat *haggis,* or when Norwegians eat *lutefisk,* they are remembering the hard times their ancestors suffered when they had to resort to eating sheep innards or cod soaked in lye. When we Americans eat turkey, mashed potatoes, cranberries, etc. for Thanksgiving, we remember God's provision for our people's ancestors. Most traditional ethnic food has some historical connection to past generations.

Culture is passed down and spread by relationships. Whoever you hang around with will influence how you act. If you have strong family relationships like the Bible portrays, then your culture, and therefore your food, will be strongly influenced by your ethnic traditions. This multi-generational culture serves as a way to honor father and mother, teach some humility and stability in our progress and growth, and call to remembrance the fact that we are part of a community that includes past generations. It helps us remember where we came from and where we are going. It keeps us humble in times of plenty and joyful in times of want.

Another time when we use food in remembrance is the Lord's Supper. When instituting it, Christ said, "Do this, as often as you drink it, in remembrance of me" (1 Cor. 11:25). It is not a coincidence that Jesus chose food for the elements by which He is to be remembered. Even more important than remembering our ancestors by food is remembering Christ by food. And just as remembering your family's or nation's history brings closer community, so in a spiritual and supernatural sense, remembering Christ's death and resurrection brings a close communion with Him and with His people. And that brings us to my next point.

Food and Communing

"The cup of blessing that we bless, is it not a participation in the blood of Christ? The bread that we break, is it not a participation in the body of

Christ? Because there is one bread, we who are many are one body, for we all partake of the one bread."
—1 Corinthians 10:16–17

The two central points to Communion are community and union. When we eat and drink the bread and wine, we participate in the body and blood of Christ. The union with the members of the body (Christians) and the head (Christ) is participated in through the sacramental food. This communion is continued until Christ's return when it is consummated in the marriage supper of the Lamb (Matt. 22:1–14; Rev. 19:9). The food is a physical sensation of nourishment and beauty that signifies the real spiritual presence of Christ who gives us life. The beauty of mixing many ingredients together into a unity of taste and nourishment is the perfect way to symbolize the beautiful union of many believers into the one body of which Christ is the head. It is no surprise that God uses food as a means of communion. Food, hospitality, and relationships are strongly connected.

"Do not neglect to show hospitality to strangers, for thereby some have entertained angels unawares" (Heb. 13:2). This passage brings to mind Abraham, who instantly provided food and rest to the three traveling strangers in Genesis 18:1-21, and indeed "entertained angels unawares." Hospitality, of which food plays a prominent part, is not merely a good idea, but it is commanded. "Contribute to the needs of the saints and seek to show hospitality" (Rom. 12:13). "Show hospitality to one another without grumbling" (1 Pet. 4:9). Hospitality is essential for good relationships and often revolves around food. Relationships form the foundation for any kind of worthwhile community and love. And if one does not love his brother, he "is not of God" (1 John 3:10).

Food is not only important in hospitality to strangers or friends, but it forms a very important part of day-to-day family life. The commandment, "Honor your father and your mother" (Exod. 20:12), is foundational to all our human relations.

> "A family is the seminary of Church and State; and if children be not well principled there, all miscarrieth … if youth be bred ill in the family, they prove ill in Church and Commonwealth."[3]

When families eat together in love, they are forming relationships and unity that build the kingdom of God. Because of our materialism, our lives use so much of our working capacity, but we ignore our thinking and loving. Some things like relationships, family, and community are not improved by industrialism and government programs. We have to get it into our minds that simple and ancient things like eating and conversing as a family are foundational to a Christian culture and society. We should spend time eating with one another. Even though it might decrease the efficiency of our work, and it won't necessarily produce material profit, it is an important and ultimate part of our life.

On this subject of food and relationships, it is important to note that the people you eat with are an indication of where your heart is. Since eating is a time of relaxing from work

---

3 Thomas Manton, "Mr. Thomas Manton's Epistle to the Reader," in *Westminster Confession of Faith* (Glasgow: Free Presbyterian Publications, 1994), 9.

and a time for fellowship, it is a sacred time for those things that you value. If you eat while watching TV, it shows that you value fellowship with what is on TV. If you grab a bite to eat during a business meeting, it shows that you value your business. If you meet your friends at McDonald's, it shows that you value your peer group. If you eat with your family, it shows that you value your family. What you value will change your culture. When people recognize that it is healthier and cheaper to make their own food at home, they still will have a hard time changing their habits. But if they value family, they will not be going hither and yonder on a regular basis because their home and hospitality will be central.

Not only does food play a part in fellowship, but fellowship also affects our attitude about food. The Bible recognizes food as being very controversial. Because it plays such an essential role in life, people get very emotionally attached to their food. They are constantly making decisions about what they eat, so when someone criticizes their diet, they are easily offended because it is so much of who they are. It is in this context that Paul says to the Corinthians: "Therefore, if food makes my brother stumble, I will never eat meat, lest I make my brother stumble." (1 Cor. 8:13) We should be wise in our food decisions, especially in hospitality. Just because we should normally eat plants and "clean" foods doesn't mean that we should wage war on those that eat pork, and it also doesn't mean that we can't eat a hot dog at our friend's picnic (1 Cor. 10:27). And just because we have the right to eat all animals doesn't mean we have to flaunt our liberty in front of those whose "conscience is weak" (1 Cor. 8:10).

> "Do not, for the sake of food, destroy the work of God. Everything is indeed clean, but it is wrong for anyone to make another stumble by what he eats."
> —Romans 14:20

> "Better is a dinner of herbs where love is than a fattened ox and hatred with it."
> —Proverbs 15:17

Food and Worshiping

This aspect of food basically sums up all the uses of food. Whether you are rejoicing, mourning, remembering, or communing, whatever you do should lead to the worship and glory of God (1 Cor. 10:31). We rejoice because of God's goodness; we mourn because of our lack of God's holiness. We remember God's providence, and we love others because He first loved us. We worship God because every good thing comes from God (James 1:17), and that includes our food.

> "Therefore I tell you, do not be anxious about your life, what you will eat or what you will drink, nor about your body, what you will put on. Is not life more than food, and the body more than clothing?"
> —Matthew 6:25

We often take food for granted in our rich society of today. We should be very careful to be thankful and not to fall into the trap of Sodom, of whom it is said,

The Christian Philosophy of Food

> "This was the guilt of your sister Sodom: she and her daughters had pride, excess of food, and prosperous ease, but did not aid the poor and needy."
> —Ezekiel 16:49

We should not forget that it is God who supplies our daily bread (Matt. 6:11), and He could take that away in a heartbeat.

We should always be thankful for the food God has given us (1 Thess. 5:18). There are some people who over-indulge in self-serving pleasures, eat only the tasty parts of food as refined and processed pleasure foods, and then take pills and powders to "balance" their diet. They are ungrateful for the balance in food God has made and seek out their own way of pleasure. There are other people who think that food is only a means to survive, and the enjoyment of food because it gives physical pleasure is unbecoming to a Christian. Instead, we should praise God for giving us tasty food that is pleasing and beautiful to our God-given senses. And there are those who over-emphasize nutrition and get caught up in strictly banning any food that might have anything detrimental to health. Unintentionally, many have become ungrateful for everything that is not perfectly healthy. Instead, even though we strive for health and nutrition, we should be grateful and content with what we receive. These several ways of being ungrateful are predicted and remedied in the Bible:

> "Now the Spirit expressly says that in later times some will depart from the faith by devoting themselves to deceitful spirits and teachings of demons, through the insincerity of liars whose consciences are seared, who

forbid marriage and require abstinence from foods that God created to be received with thanksgiving by those who believe and know the truth. For everything created by God is good, and nothing is to be rejected if it is received with thanksgiving, for it is made holy by the word of God and prayer."

–1 Timothy 4:1–5

The food we eat is made holy. It is set apart for righteousness by the Word of God and prayer. This is because if we are consistent as Christians, we will eat for God's glory with thanksgiving to Him. When that is done, we will not be either "health-obsessed" or sensuously self-centered. We will thank God for making His food healthy and tasty in perfect balance and moderation. We will stand in awe of His wisdom in His creation, and we will not pervert His blessings for our glory.

Four

FOOD AND ECONOMICS

But wait, there's more! Because food is one of the basic needs of life and takes much effort to produce, food production and preparation have been basic to economics and work throughout time. Tending the garden was the primary work given to Adam and Eve. Abraham, Isaac, Jacob, Moses, David, and many others in the Bible raised sheep. Much of the work of the Israelites was in agriculture; many of the Apostles were originally fishermen, and Jesus Himself made extensive use of farming illustrations in His parables. Not only is food production a basic component of work, but how we work with food affects our food, our health, and our culture. In fact, economics and work can be viewed as a subset of culture. Therefore I cannot ignore this important part of the Christian philosophy of food.

WHY WORK?
Serving God or Serving Man

Why do we work? Many people today (at least in America) when asked this question will answer that they work to provide sustenance to live on. Work for many is seen as a necessary evil that is only done to provide income for one's self, or perhaps for one's family. This is because,

> "[N]ot only work but life apart from God is meaningless. Work then becomes a question of survival economics, gaining enough food and shelter to live. For all too many people in history, work has had this connotation. Its goal has been survival, and hence it has had a sad and burdensome aura. Escape from work is then a much desired goal."[1]

If people get a chance not to work, they retire (which often involves the government in some way) and take the opportunity to live a life of leisure. Perhaps they travel across the country in a RV, buy a house in Florida, or simply sit and watch TV, but why keep working when you don't have to? Yes, we can see examples and principles from the Bible such as in Deuteronomy 14:22–29 where there is a time for celebration and rest that is a great blessing (besides the Lord's Day); therefore vacations and rest from work are not sins *per se*. But this is not to be the end goal of work or the ideal state of life because that would deprive us of the joy and blessing of work. The idea of a grandfather working with his son and grandson like in the TV show *The Waltons,* or even to be the wise and respected mentor of the next generation, is thought of as being outdated and foreign. I am not saying that those individuals who have retired are any guiltier than the rest of us since our culture is one of youth and the new, and the corporate model of work is built that way. But it is indicative

---

1 Rousas John Rushdoony, *Systematic Theology,* (Vallecito, CA: Ross House Books, 1994), 2: 1020.

that as a culture we view work in a wrong way. We have lost the paradigm that work is a divine ordinance and a form of worship. In the Bible, God gave Adam work before the Fall, hence it preceded evil and sin.

> "The LORD God took the man and put him in the garden of Eden to work it and keep it."
> —Genesis 2:15

Therefore work is not evil, but it is good and something to delight in. It must be noted that our work is harder now because of sin (Gen. 3:17–19), but that doesn't mean that work is evil. Any difficulty in the work we have that comes from the Curse is only a small taste of what we *should* be getting for our sin. Even the curse is a blessing, in that it reminds us of our sinfulness. Work is not the problem; our sin is the problem. Throughout Scripture is the command to work. "Six days you shall labor, and do all your work" (Exod. 20:9).

> "For even when we were with you, we would give you this command: If anyone is not willing to work, let him not eat.
> For we hear that some among you walk in idleness, not busy at work, but busybodies. Now such persons we command and encourage in the Lord Jesus Christ to do their work quietly and to earn their own living."
> —2 Thessalonians 3:10–12

"But if anyone does not provide for his relatives, and especially for members of his household, he has denied the faith and is worse than an unbeliever."
—1 Timothy 5:8

"Slaves, obey your earthly masters with fear and trembling, with a sincere heart, as you would Christ, not by the way of eye-service, as people-pleasers, but as servants of Christ, doing the will of God from the heart, rendering service with a good will as to the Lord and not to man."
—Ephesians 6:5–7

Our lives are lives of worship. Everything we do is an act of worshiping something. We do things because of what we value. We might work because we worship comfort and therefore work for material well-being. We might worship progress and change themselves, working to make all things new over and over again. We might even worship humanity, working to provide for people in a purely humanistic fashion. If we worship God, we work to fulfill God's commands in Scripture to "fill the earth and subdue it" (Gen. 1:28) for His glory, and we labor to provide for others out of love. If we work for God, our goal should be nothing less than excellence. This gives zest to labor and serves to measure the degree of success. We toil, not merely to obtain sustenance, but to produce excellent things for the glory of God.

> "The world does not consider labor a blessing, therefore, it flees and hates it but the pious who fear the Lord, labor with a ready and cheerful heart; for they

know God's command and will, they acknowledge His calling."[2]

—Martin Luther

Richard M. Weaver stated it well in his book *Ideas Have Consequences:*

"When Utilitarianism becomes enthroned and the worker is taught that work is use and not worship, interest in quality begins to decline. How many times have we heard exclamations of wonder at the care which went into some article of ancient craftsmanship before modern organization drove a wedge between the worker and his product! There is the difference between expressing one's self in form and producing quantity for a market with an eye to speculation. Peguy wished to know what had become of the honor of work. It has succumbed to the same forces as have all other expressions of honor."[3]

Perhaps this says something about the economic problems of today. We can see for sure that a nation that fears the Lord will be blessed with many good workers. Let us remember that the government cannot save us from economic woes—only the fear and love of God can do that.

---

2 George Grant & Karen Grant, *Lost Causes* (Nashville, TN: Cumberland House Publishing, Inc. 1999), 36.

3 Richard M. Weaver, *Ideas Have Consequences* (Chicago and London: University of Chicago Press, 1984), 73–74.

How Do We Work?
Family Economy vs. Corporation

Throughout the Bible, families worked together. Adam and Eve worked together to tend the garden. In one of the earliest instances of economics, we see multi-generation families as economic units.

> "Adah bore Jabal; he was the father of those who dwell in tents and have livestock. His brother's name was Jubal; he was the father of all those who play the lyre and pipe."
> —Genesis 4:20–21

Rachel tended her father's sheep. The households of the Patriarchs worked together. David tended his father's sheep. James and John were in a boat with their father when Jesus called them to be Apostles. Aquila and Priscilla were tentmakers together.

The concept of the corporation, in which the fathers (and/or mothers for that matter) leave the family to work for an organization other than the family, is foreign to Scripture. There are four jurisdictions found in the Bible: the Individual, the Family, the Church, and the State. Economics (from the Greek word oikonomia: *oîkos* = house, *nomos* = law) and business are in the jurisdiction of the family. While private corporations are not sinful *per se*, they are not the Biblical ideal and can have bad consequences on the rest of life by dividing the family. The wife is to be a helpmeet to her husband. Having two different visions of work in a family tends to divide it, and a house divided will not stand (Mark

3:25). This is not only true if the mom and dad both go to their own businesses; it is also true in the "traditional family" where the mom raises the kids, and the dad supplies the finances by laboring at some workplace unrelated to the rest of the family (and the kids don't produce anything). For a family to be united and to be a viable relational unit, it must have a unified vision of work. Life is an organic thing. The different parts of life are interconnected, and what you do in one part will affect the rest. Work is not something you can separate from the rest of life, and who you work with will determine your firmest relationships. In Genesis 2:24 it does not say that "a man should leave his father and his mother and hold fast to his" corporation, business, or government, and "they shall become one flesh." What it does say is,

> "Therefore a man shall leave his father and his mother and hold fast to his wife, and they shall become one flesh."
> −Genesis 2:24[4]

What Does This Have to Do with Food?
Food as Part of the Family Economy

So we are to work for God's glory, primarily as families. While it might seem like we may have wandered from our subject of food, food is an important part of our work (as I said at the beginning of this chapter). Today, food has been separated from the family. It used to be that families grew their food, cooked at home, and ate together. Then later in

---

4 For more teaching on family economics, Generations with Vision has some great resources on this subject at http://generationswithvision.com/Store.

history children went to school and fathers went to work, so the mothers would pack lunches. Then the fathers and children started eating at the cafeterias, and mothers went to work—or they got frozen food and watched soap operas. The idea of the family being an integral part of food production has suffered a great deal.

It is thought that if we follow government guidelines for eating, then everything will be fine. But, even besides the fact that business (including agriculture) is primarily in the jurisdiction of the family, the civil government (especially our massive centralized government) cannot know the specifics of each person's situation. If government agencies make a mistake, the consequences are vastly multiplied. And when the government proclaims that everyone has a "right" to healthy food and artificially subsidizes certain foods that there isn't a demand for, it only increases waste. It is simply not the civil government's responsibility to regulate our diets.

In the private sector as well, it is argued that having specialized and centralized systems of food production and distribution is more efficient and requires less labor. But it is an efficiency that sacrifices quality and character. Again, quality food that is good for us is not valued today as much as pleasure and ease. But if our work is a form of worship to God, and food is a source of health to our God-given temples of the Holy Spirit, and it is an expression of our worship and being, then maybe we should value the time we spend working with food. And, despite its claims of efficiency, centralized food production is actually just as prone to food waste, albeit in different ways.[5] Not only do mistakes happen on a greater scale, but when the average consumer is removed from the production, the work put into it is not well-respected. Thus, consumers in industrialized countries waste food more often than consumers in developing countries.[6] When you work for your food and see the effort put into it, you will be more careful with the way you use it. And then, even if the big businesses are more efficient, to survive and grow they must seek as their goal the satisfaction of the masses, even if the masses are addicted to poor choices. Thus it is natural for them to gravitate to the lowest common denominator in making food, at the same time making the people desire that food even more. The unhealthy wants of the people and the power of centralized business go together to make a downward spiral of unhealthy eating that is hard to break.

Not only are the centralized and statist systems not the Biblical method, but their consequences are destructive to society (not a surprise). The systems are not the starting point of the problem, but instead it is the man-centered worldview including centralization and materialism that destroys society. This is opposite to what a Biblical worldview produces in society.

---

5 Jenny Gustavsson, et al. "Global Food Losses and Food Waste" (Food and Agriculture Organization of the United Nations, 2011), 5, http://www.fao.org/fileadmin/user_upload/ags/publications/GFL_web.pdf.

6 Ibid.

Take for example the woman in Proverbs 31:

> "She is like the ships of the merchant;
> she brings her food from afar.
> She rises while it is yet night
> and provides food for her household
> and portions for her maidens."
> —Proverbs 31:14–15

She provides food, not for her corporation or government, but for her household. She works with and for people who she is in relationship with and genuinely cares for. There is no economic stimulus better than love. Even if a family doesn't grow its own food, when family members work to at least cook their own food, there will be much more care and quality put into it than when it is made by an employee working for pay. When a family works together to care for one another, it is working as a viable social-economic unit.

Our God is a relational God because He is the Trinitarian God who spends eternity enjoying His Own interpersonal fellowship, and it is because of His relational love that we have love for one another (John 17). In a Biblical culture life would be centered much more on loving relationships (Mal. 4:6; Gal. 6:10; 1 John 3:16–17, 4:7–21), and it thus would be centered more on the family and local community where relationships have time to grow. Just as families are made up of interconnected individuals, communities are based on interconnected families (Exod. 20:12; Neh. 7:7–60; Ps. 22:27). In 1 Thessalonians 4:9–12 it says to the brothers in

Thessalonica to love one another, live quietly, and work so that they might "be dependent on no one." It is not saying that each individual is to fend for himself. The Bible teaches that we are to care for one another and to live in community (Acts 2:42–47). This passage is teaching that the local community, especially the household of faith (Gen. 6:10), should be largely self-sufficient, not dependent on the outsiders who they are to "walk properly before" (1 Thess. 4:12). Thus families do not have to be totally self-sufficient, and everything does not have to be done by single families. But when families work together in the local community, the families and households are the fundamental units that work together, rather than the corporation being the fundamental unit that individuals work for. In a Biblical model, work would be centered around real relational community that is integrated into life and family.

This decentralized and relational method of economics applies to agriculture and cooking—two things that were more important for families in the past than they are today, and which were important in ancient Hebrew culture and historic Christendom.

Agriculture

Agriculture is more than producing crops and livestock. It is a direct and basic way of taking dominion over creation and interacting with God's created order. As Noah Webster said in his 1828 dictionary, "Agriculture is the most general occupation of man."[7] The words *agriculture* and *cultivation*

[7] *Noah Webster's 1828 American Dictionary,* 1828., s.v. "Agriculture," accessed December 2, 2011,
http://www.1828-dictionary.com/d/search/word,agriculture

come from the same Latin root word as *culture, cultured,* and *cult: colere* (or *colō,* meaning to till, cultivate, nurture, honor, or worship). When someone cultivates the land, he shows faith in God's providence and hope for the future. He is directly making civilization out of wilderness and working in God's creation for its improvement. As we will explore in the next chapter, by interacting closely with creation, we learn God's "eternal power and divine nature." (Rom. 1:20) The benefits of agriculture are many, as E. C. Wines says in his book *The Hebrew Republic:*

> "The physical and moral influences of agriculture ought not to be overlooked.... It is the nurse of health, industry, temperance, cheerfulness and frugality; of simple manners and pure morals; of patriotism and the domestic virtues; and, above all, of that sturdy independence, without which a man is not a man, but the mere slave, or plaything, of his more cunning fellows. Agriculture tends to produce and cherish a spirit of equality and sympathy.... Agriculture begets and strengthens love of country. The heart of the husbandman is bound to the fields, on which he bestows his labor. The soil, which responds to his industry by clothing itself in beauty and riches, has a place in his affections. Especially, the circumstance, that his possession has come down to him through a long line of honored ancestors, greatly strengthens the

attachment, which he feels to his home and county [see Numbers 33:54 and Leviticus 25:23]....

"... It is in the scenes and occupations of country life, that the mind is most tranquil, sober, and unclouded. It is in such an atmosphere, that it can discern most clearly the relations of things, and look beyond the events of a day... In a word this great business, the cultivation of the earth, lies, so far as any branch of human industry can be said to lie, at the foundation of all that is important and valuable in civil society."[8]

There can be much said about agriculture from a Biblical perspective. Some things must wait for the next chapter where I will discuss our view towards God's creation in general, but a few things should be pointed out here.

Because "The earth is the LORD's" (Ps. 24:1), we must follow God's directions when it comes to using His land. In Leviticus 19:9–10 we are told,

"You shall not reap your field right up to its edge, neither shall you gather the gleanings after your harvest...You shall leave them for the poor and for the sojourner."

God's plan of charity includes a certain amount of inefficiency in farming. This way the poor still have to work some to get food by collecting the leftovers, but they are still provided

---

8 E.C. Wines, *The Hebrew Republic* (Uxbridge, MA: American Presbyterian Press, 1980), 11f, quoted in Joseph Morecraft III, *Authentic Christianity* (Powder Springs, GA: Minkoff Family Publishing & American Vision 2009), 616–617.

for by farmers in the local community. Eventually the poor would get better at working and would be able to get back on their feet. Simple handouts by the impersonal state are no replacement for this kind of charity. Another law that is important to note is the seventh year rest for the land (found in Exod. 23:10–11 and Lev. 25:1–7). In it the land is left alone without planting, pruning, or harvesting. Remember when we talked about how man needs rest? So does the land if it is to be fertile and healthy. This rest in the seventh year requires that the farmer think ahead of time to plan for it. Also, for it to be true rest, the farmer must have faith in God's provision. The same can be said for his weekly rest on the Lord's Day and his nightly rest in bed. A third thing to point out that is very important in agriculture and economics in general is the Bible's protection of private property as a safeguard of the liberty of the family. In the Bible there is no tax on the land, and no one can steal the land, including the government (1 Kings 21). There are many laws protecting the ownership and inheritance of land contributing to the strength and stability of the family economy (Exod. 20:15 & 17; Lev. 25:13, 23–24; Prov. 13:22). There are other directions in the Bible concerning agriculture (Lev. 19:23–25; Deut. 25:4; 2 Tim. 2:6; etc.), but these are some of the main ones that we have forgotten and should follow if we are to farm for the glory of God.

When God redeems a person, it doesn't just affect his isolated self, but he is also sanctified in his relations to other people and the world around him. When a person loves God, he lives more and more according to God's law, and that law acts as a blessing to his personal relationships, society, and environment. As Adam's sin resulted in the land being cursed, so Christ's redemption results in the renewal of the land, culminating in the fully-restored new heaven and earth at Christ's return. Christ is in the process of "making all things new" (Rev. 21:5), and we are part of that as we take responsible dominion of creation.

Now this isn't to say that we must all become farmers. There are other ways to work and take dominion. But it is to say that in a Biblical society, agriculture will be much more widespread and general in the society rather than being an elite centralized system (like we have now) where only 1% of the population farm. Even if the main source of income is not farming, the work of gardening to supplement the food supply, or even for the sake of learning how God's creation works, will be important. The more a family knows where its food comes from, the more accountability and incentive for quality will be evident in agriculture. When people grow their crops with faith in God and love for those who will eat the food, while working for His glory, the land will be blessed with hard workers who will produce good food that has been nourished by God's good Providence.

Cooking

As agriculture is not just the production of plants, cooking is not just making stuff edible. Cooking is a process by which raw materials are cultivated into a work of art to be eaten by people we love, people who are made in the image of God. This is especially true when done in a relational community like the family. As Christians, our cooking ideally should not be hastily-made slop, but instead our food should reflect God's nature and glory by being beautiful.

God is beautiful. He loves beauty and actually defines beauty. Beauty is part of His nature. "For how great is his goodness, and how great his beauty!" (Zech. 9:17a, see also Ps. 27:4, 50:2) What constitutes beauty has been the subject of much discussion over the years, but even humanist philosophers have perceived certain patterns in creation that are more pleasing than others. Beauty can be described as that which is composed of things in the right proportion to each other. A common way to describe beauty has been something like the old definition of the Roman School, "multitude in unity."[9] The Enlightenment philosopher Francis Hutcheson observed,

> "The Figures which excite in us the Ideas of Beauty, seem to be those in which there is Uniformity amidst Variety."[10]

While the terms describing beauty vary depending on what aspect of life is being looked at, they are different terms for the same ultimate values that are found in the definition of beauty Himself, the Triune God. God is one Being subsisting

---

9 *Webster's Revised Unabridged Dictionary 1913.*, s.v. "Beauty," accessed December 2, 2011, http://1913.mshaffer.com/d/word/beauty.

10 Francis Hutcheson, "SECTION II: Of Original or Absolute Beauty. Part III," in *An Inquiry into the Original of Our Ideas of Beauty and Virtue in Two Treatises,* ed. Wolfgang Leidhold (Indianapolis: Liberty Fund, 2004), accessed December 2, 2011,
http://oll.libertyfund.org/?option=com_staticxt&staticfile=show.php%3Ftitle=858&chapter=65974&layout=html#a_1607960.

in three persons (God the Father, God the Son, and God the Holy Spirit).

> "In God's being, there are no individual persons not perfectly related to the one God; and there is nothing in the whole being of God that is not fully expressed in the three, distinct persons."[11]

In God's Being, neither the one God nor the several Persons are more important or ultimate, but in His Being both the One and the Particular are equally God. God made His creation to reflect the way He is (Rom. 1:19–20), and thus beauty in God and in creation is the balance between the ultimate values of unity and diversity. They are by no means opposing ideas, but they are instead complementary values that cannot have meaning without each other. Without recognizing diversity in reality, the universal becomes meaningless sameness, and without recognizing unity in reality, the particularities become meaningless and unrelated. The first is static; the other is chaotic. When referring to art I find the terms *order* and *zeal* the best for showing the distinct but not separate parts of beauty. Cooking, as well as music, dance, poetry, and other art forms, involves both.

The Unity of Order

Music teaches unified order through its orderly and mathematical beat, scales, and intervals. In dance there are steps in concert with the order of the music, and the dancers are in order with the other dancers. There are sometimes

---

[11] Joseph Morecraft III, *Authentic Christianity* (Powder Springs, GA: Minkoff Family Publishing & American Vision, 2009), 387.

complex tunes and steps, but they must fit with the order. We seem to be by nature chaotic, sporadic, and random. For example, people do not naturally walk in beat. Meals do not grow as meals. For the meal to be beautiful, the food needs to be harvested, washed, put together, seasoned, and oftentimes heated. We must work to produce food that is orderly, clean, and composed of ingredients in unity and right proportion to each other. Orderly art trains nature to conform to order and regularity. It teaches self-control and self-discipline that submits our bodies, thoughts, actions, and life to God's peace and harmony. As 1 Corinthians 14:33 says, "For God is not a God of confusion but of peace." And as 1 Corinthians 14:40 says, "All things should be done decently and in order." We truly take dominion over and cultivate God's creation when we shape it according to God's orderliness. When we learn to act according to orderliness and peace, we are acting according to the nature of God.

The Particularity of Zeal

But of course orderliness is not the only thing that our cooking requires, since then our food would be bland and boring. Beauty is not static or dull; it has life and character. God is a God of love and zeal. Isaiah 42:13 says, "The Lord goes out like a mighty man, like a man of war he stirs up his zeal." Isaiah 59:17 describes the Lord wrapping himself "in zeal as a cloak." Romans 12:11 commands, "Do not be slothful in zeal, be fervent in spirit." We are not to be dry and monotonous people, but people with fervent love and joy. Our food should have life. It should have interesting variations of taste and texture. It should refresh and enliven. It should have variety and alternating expressions of crispness and smoothness, hot and cold, and sweet and savory. But of course we should mix it with order. If we only have zeal, that zeal will become chaotic and will lose meaning. Let our food not be like a bunch of people shouting "I love you!" at the top of their lungs, but let it be like a beautifully crafted song of love with melody and harmony.

Pop Food

Using the comparison of cooking and music, one can see how modern food is much like modern music. It has the same substance—a deficient, commercialized, always "new and improved" character about it. Much of our food is Pop food. Just like Pop music, it is a product of the mix of Romanticism, which emphasized the emotions at the expense of rules and order, Industrialism, which emphasized commercial interests and mass appeal, and Modernism, which emphasized the new and different.[12] As people get more hooked on Pop art, by the nature of it, they get drawn into the spiral of demanding the next grand excitement which must stimulate them more than the last. It actually corrupts taste and recognition of what is good. After we have become accustomed to Pop music, listening to Bach seems boring, difficult, and distasteful, much like eating vegetables. To many people it seems that healthy foods always taste bad. Now that we are used to foods crammed with sugar and salt, going back to a more delicate and balanced diet of plants, flavored with herbs and spices,

12 Kenneth A. Myers, *All God's Children and Blue Suede Shoes* (Wheaton, IL: Crossway Books, 1989), 139–140.

seems like listening to Handel after having listened to rap for your entire life. Healthy food actually tastes good! It is our tastes that have been corrupted through the unrestrained pursuit of stimulation. It takes a while, but when you start eating healthfully on a regular basis, the appreciation for the rich diversity of tastes grows and become a delight. Not only that, but eating Pop foods is then as repulsive as if you were a classical musician listening to heavy metal. The other related consideration is that a rap artist will not play Handel's *Messiah* very well the first time. When a person or a culture is not used to cooking vegetables, it will take some practice to learn how cook them right (e.g. not overcooking them to a mush).

And finally, not only is the food to be beautiful, but the whole atmosphere of the meal should be one of love and order of a Godly family. While in reality life does not always allow for the opportunity of a peaceful and loving family meal, this should be our goal to strive for. In a perfect world the food would be lovingly prepared by the family, for the family, and perhaps for other families. Because the food would be made locally and relationally, there would be more accountability in the process. There would be local character and special attention in the food that would otherwise be swallowed up by corporate management. The family would enjoy a break from the day's labor and have enjoyable fellowship around the table, discussing the day's lessons and trials. The food would inspire an atmosphere of familial love and orderliness that would grow into the rest of the experience. The more beautiful the food is, the more beautiful the experience of fellowship will be. The more beautiful the food, the more we can fully glorify God and enjoy Him and His perfect beauty.

Five

FOOD AND THE CREATION

As I said in the introduction, food is part of creation, and our view of creation will affect how we look at food. Because God created the world (Gen. 1–2), we regard the world in terms of God's purposes and order. When God created man, God made him as one who exercises dominion.

> "This is not something peripheral to man's being: it is essential to his nature. Either man will exercise a godly dominion or an evil, humanistic one."[1]

While man is not a robot that simply produces and does nothing else, this aspect of man's nature cannot be ignored. Man is a creature; he is part of God's creation and cannot escape his part in that creation. When we mess up our view of creation and our responsible part in it, our relation to it and its produce will be skewed and detrimental to our lives.

Autonomous and rebellious man wants to escape the God who judges. Because the creation is God's, he is in a hostile environment and thus regards nature as something of an

1 Rushdoony, *Systematic Theology*, 961.

enemy. Because he is proud of his human abilities, he thinks that the science and reason of man will save him, and that creation can all be comprehended and remade into perfection. On the other hand, there are other ungodly men who react strongly against this position of reason and science, instead taking the path of natural primitivism.

The Romantics had the same kind of reaction to the Enlightenment philosophers in the 1800s. During the Enlightenment, the philosophers elevated the particular through rationalism (knowledge through reason) and empiricism (knowledge through the senses). They reduced life to science and natural processes.[2] The Romantics reacted to this by elevating feeling, instinct, irrationality, and emotion. At the expense of the diversity of observation and reason, they emphasized the oneness of nature and feeling.[3] Because both the Rationalists/Empiricists and the Romantics had wandered from a correct understanding of the Biblical Trinity, they swung from one extreme to another, neither one being Biblically defined.

---

[2] Of course, they had to assume some kind of unity to hold their observations together or else they fell into skepticism.

[3] Because of the nature of emotions and nature the Romantics still had to recognize some kind of diversity, but it was often subsumed into a oneness of nature in a pantheistic way. As R. W. Emerson explained his relation to nature, "Standing on the bare ground, — my head bathed by the blithe air, and uplifted into infinite space, — all mean egotism vanishes. I become a transparent eye-ball; I am nothing; I see all; the currents of the Universal Being circulate through me; I am part or particle of God." (Ralph Waldo Emerson, *Nature,* 1836, accessed December 2, 2011, http://www.vcu.edu/engweb/transcendentalism/authors/emerson/essays/naturetext.html).

Food and the Creation

In our own time we have seen a reaction against the humanistic scientists, starting with the hippies and continuing in related groups today. Many liberals have recognized the futility of scientific naturalism and industrialism, so they have instead concluded that since mankind is unable to fully comprehend and control the processes of life, he cannot know anything and should return to primitive irrationality. They deny the particulars of creation, or at least man's ability to understand them, claiming that any attempt on the part of humans to improve it is bound to only corrupt it. The more organic, natural, and untouched by the hand of man the better. This reaction seems good at first because it recognizes the problem correctly. The direction they head at first is in the same direction that Christians take, but because they deny God they are unable to balance diversity and unity, erring on the side of unity.[4]

As opposed to the ungodly, Christians worship the Triune God. We are the only ones who can correctly balance a right view of creation because we serve the Creator. We understand that God is a God of order, and that we are made in the image of God, so thus we are able to understand some of the patterns of nature that originate with God's orderly nature. This gives meaning to the particulars of reason and science. But we also realize that man is a finite and created being, not to mention one who has been corrupted by sin. While there are things that we can know from general and special revelation (God's creation and His Scriptures), we are limited. There are things that are mysteries to us. When we approach God and His

---

[4] This is how Eastern mysticism has become a part of the natural foods movement.

The Christian Philosophy of Food

creation, we should do so with fear and humility. Instead of relying on science to remake creation into a man-made utopia, we should use it to uncover the value of what exists in God's creation, thereby working as His stewards to subdue and improve creation to reflect God's nature and sanctifying power. Instead of viewing God's creation as an enemy or a god, we view it as God's garden that we are to carefully tend and make beautiful and bountiful.

Part of viewing creation as God's garden is recognizing the imprint of God's nature and character in His creation. Because of man's sinful nature, he suppresses the natural revelation of God through His creation, being unable to properly interpret it. However, as Christians who know and love the Creator and who study His Word, we can see God's truth illustrated in His creation. One example of this is God allowing the sun to rise and the rain to fall on the evil and good, just and unjust. It should be clear from this aspect of God's creation that we should also love our enemies and pray for those who persecute us (Matt. 5:44–45). Delicious and nourishing foods are benefits of sun and rain that are available to all. That does not mean that all appreciate it and delight in it as a miraculous design for their benefit. As people turn from God, they lose respect for God's wisdom in creation and pervert it. This apostasy has been made plain to us as we see nations turn from God, becoming obese and suffering from associated diseases. Healthy populations in the past who have not had access to an abundance of indulgent foods (e.g. people on the island of Okinawa) serve as an example of the common blessings that God provides to people in His created

FOOD AND THE CREATION

food. God made His creation so that it is possible for the ungodly to eat healthfully. However, the ungodly have wrong motives and do not glorify God in their choices. As children of God, it is an incredible blessing to recognize God's creation for what it is, a precious gift designed in infinite wisdom and power for our benefit. Therefore we glorify and praise God when we are good stewards of the nutrients that He provides in food by the way we learn to prepare it, serve it, and delight in it with others in Christ's love.

From experience we have learned that both the sweet and bitter components of food are gloriously made for our benefit. Though people might want to remove the bitter and astringent compounds to make food more appealing, those bitter and astringent compounds are very valuable to our bodies, actually adding richness to the taste. They can remind us of God's judgment which may seem bitter and harsh. But when we recognize God's sovereignty and goodness, we can see that even His judgment is a good thing. Without it we lose the illustration of His holy power and the riches of His glory to us (Rom. 9:22–23). Just as food deprived of "unpleasant" compounds produces an appealing and yet deficient food, so the Gospel without God's sovereignty and holiness is "seeker-friendly" but woefully lacking and weak.

The more we study food, the more we learn that every food has a special value for people. Different foods are good sources of different proteins, minerals, vitamins, fibers, fats, flavonoids, flavors, colors, etc. Foods are not homogenous, but each has a different specialty and importance that is different than the rest. To eat a healthy diet, we can't just rely on one food, but we should instead value a diversity of foods that work together, each supplying what the others are missing. This is a great picture of the body of believers. Each member of the body has his own part to play in the unity of the body. "For just as the body is one and has many members, and all the members of the body, though many, are one body, so it is with Christ.... But as it is, God arranged the members in the body, each one of them, as he chose. If all were a single member where would the body be? As it is, there are many parts, yet one body" (1 Cor. 12:12, 18–20). Though we have equal importance, we have different positions and responsibilities. This design in food is a great example of God's social order and plan for community. We can be confident from this example in His created food that He also makes every one of us for a purpose to bring Him glory.

If you have ever worked to grow a garden or raise animals for food, it does not take long to learn that it takes a lot of work to be productive. There is a difference between raising rats and raising cows, or between raising thistles and raising tomatoes. These observations of creation illustrate the teaching of God's Word that as a result of Adam's sin in the Garden of Eden,

> "In pain you shall eat of it [the ground] all the days of your life; thorns and thistles it shall bring forth for you; and you shall eat the plants of the field. By the sweat of your face you shall eat bread, till you return to the ground."
>
> —Genesis 3:17–18

Food and the Creation

We are constantly reminded of all the vast consequences of our sin by our interactions with God's once perfect creation. We are reminded that we have made God's blessing a painful one.

God created foods to grow best in different geographies; consider salmon, sea bass, coffee beans, cocoa beans, tea leaves, coconuts, pineapples, blueberries, peaches, pecans, cabbages, dry beans, grapes, and figs. This design helps us to appreciate that God knew from the beginning that the world would have these different climates, so He designed the genetic potential to adapt to them. The dramatic changes in the world at the time of the Great Flood were not a surprise. The dispersion of the different foods mirrors the dispersion of the human race from the tower of Babel. It gives each tribe, tongue, and nation its own characteristic foods, which serve to give local character to the relational community. This difference also helps to keep each people from boasting in its food, instead building appreciation for other cultures. God is sovereign, and He keeps people from being as arrogant as they could be by His design. "For from him and through him and to him are all things. To him be the glory forever. Amen." (Rom. 11:36)

As was said earlier, there is order and diversity, and thus beauty, in food that reflects God's character. One cannot escape this obvious fact when reviewing a farmers' market display of foods or by studying the details of each food. This detail of order and diversity never ends as we look at the visible, microscopic, molecular, and atomic structure of food. The design of food is undeniably incredible. Beware of people who do not humbly work with food and instead oversimplify it. It is easy to isolate a component of a food and declare that that is all you need, so you should consume it as a supplement and forget the rest of the food. Likewise it is also easy to isolate a component of a food and declare that the component is bad for you, so therefore you should avoid the food source. The different molecules and compounds of food work together in a way that is difficult to measure. The parts that are good by themselves are usually even better combined with other parts, and those that might usually be bad by themselves can interact at low levels with other parts to produce a good effect. Over time many compounds or attributes of foods that were originally considered as detrimental have not been confirmed as such; some were even found to be healthful (e.g. protease inhibitors). We see things dimly and imperfectly, especially when we study God's creation without acknowledging that He exists and has infinite wisdom and power.

In Romans 1:20 we learn that God's "invisible attributes, namely, his eternal power and divine nature, have been clearly perceived, ever since the creation of the world, in the things that have been made." A benefit of studying God's created food is the joy of discovering the attributes of God. God's infinite creativity and sovereignty are seen in the remarkable design of His creation that considers many things at one time. Just think, God designed what each plant needs to grow and survive under various climates and conditions of pests, diseases, soils, and pollinators. He also decided what nutrients each type of food should provide for us. He designed how components of food would react during cooking to create a pleasant taste or improve their usefulness to the body, and He designed how complementary foods can taste good when combined or consumed together in a meal. He designed how these nutrients are transported and transformed into different structures in the stomach, intestinal tract, bloodstream, organs, and cells, designing how the resulting structures interact with receptors, enzymes, and other molecules to benefit our bodies. Even within one type of seed is a genetic potential designed by God for a great diversity of varieties that can be selected for different times and needs that He knew would be valuable for people from the beginning of time. As the need for a greater abundance of food increased, God provided man with the will and ability to select plants that yield more food. It is incredible to see how breeders progressively increase the yield of crops decade after decade with seemingly no end in potential for even higher yields. Praise God for providing this potential in His creation. All these things He considered according to the needs of each time in history.

Oh how infinite and eternal is the power of God! He is God; we are not. He is worthy of praise, honor, and glory forever. Man in his autonomous wisdom does only what leads to death and destruction. Praise God for the examples that we see of the futility of man's destructive ways so we can realize all the more our dependence on God and the privilege of being His children through the work of Jesus Christ on the cross. Let us repent, put off the old self, and be progressively transformed to be more like Him in love, joy, peace, patience, kindness, goodness, faithfulness, gentleness, and self-control.

The Christian Philosophy of Food

Conclusion

As I come to the end of this book I feel that there is so much more to write on the various aspects of food. But as I have been writing I have also realized how interconnected these are, and how hard it is to deal with the different aspects separately. The way we work with food will influence its healthfulness. The way we view creation will influence how we work with food. The quality and nutrition of our food will influence the overall setting and culture of the meal. The way we cook food influences its healthfulness and expression. Our culture of food will influence how much we value it. So when you see that I have a chapter on an aspect of food, realize that the same aspect will occur throughout the rest of the book. This is the reason for building a Christian worldview for all of life. Life is a connected web of related subjects, and when one part is wrong, it influences the rest of life.

> "Do you not know that a little leaven leavens the whole lump? Cleanse out the old leaven that you may be a new lump, as you really are unleavened."
> —1 Corinthians 5:6b–7a

The Christian Philosophy of Food

This book has been an attempt to address food as a part of life that has not been addressed by Christians as much as, say, politics. Regrettably, conservative Bible Belt Christians have been known for unhealthy greasy eating, to our disgrace. It is time that we wake from our slumbers of comfort and start eating by the grace of God in a Biblical fashion that reflects well on the honor of Christianity, enabling us to accomplish the rest of our life in a beautiful and healthy manner. It is no easy matter. We should pray that we exhibit the fruit of the Spirit by self-control in our life and diet, that we love the beauty that reflects God's nature, that we are given a will to work in love for God and man, and that we carefully use and enjoy God's world for His glory alone. This is not something we can do on our own, but it will only come from God's working in us for our sanctification.

When we have a proper view of food, it will help us to have a correct view of God. As Jesus says in Matthew 4:4, "Man shall not live by bread alone, but by every word that comes from the mouth of God." As food sustains our bodies and gives us life, so in the ultimate sense we are given eternal life through "the word of life" (Phil. 2:16). And in John 6:35,

> "Jesus said to them, 'I am the bread of life; whoever comes to me shall not hunger, and whoever believes in me shall never thirst.'"

In Jesus we are fulfilled, and in him we lack nothing. Just as a good meal will fill you up for a time and give you enjoyment and thankfulness, so Jesus fills us for eternity, and in Him we find full enjoyment and thankfulness. God is often referred

Conclusion

to as life-giving, cleansing, and refreshing water (Isa. 44:2–5; Jer. 17:13; John 4:10; etc.). When our food is beautiful and nutritious, it helps us remember better that we have a great and almighty God.

The end of the matter is this: God is almighty and God is good. God has given us great food to explore and enjoy, and He has given us the way to enjoy it. Oh, peoples of the earth, "taste and see that the Lord is good!" (Ps. 34:8) Give God glory and honor for Who He is and for His wonderful works that he has blessed us with, and never take His blessings for granted. Let us love Him and eat His way, by His power, and for His glory.

> "So, whether you eat or drink, or whatever you do, do all to the glory of God."
> —1 Corinthians 10:31

Bibliography

Calvin, John. "Commentary on Corinthians." Accessed December 2, 2011. http://www.ccel.org/ccel/calvin/calcom39.xiii.iii.html.

Calvin, John. *Institutes of the Christian Religion.* trans. Henry Beveridge Peabody, MA: Hendrickson Publishers, Inc., 2008

Eshel, Gidon, & Pamela A Martin. "Geophysics and nutritional science: towards a novel, unified paradigm." The American Journal of Clinical Nutrition 89 (suppl) (2009): 1710S–6S.

Grant, George & Karen. *Lost Causes.* Nashville, TN: Cumberland House Publishing, Inc., 1999

Gustavsson, Jenny, et al., "Global Food Losses and Food Waste," Food and Agriculture Organization of the United Nations (2011). Accessed December 19, 2011. http://www.fao.org/fileadmin/user_upload/ags/publications/GFL_web.pdf.

Hutcheson, Francis. "SECTION II: Of Original or Absolute Beauty. Part III," In *An Inquiry into the Original of Our Ideas of Beauty and Virtue in Two Treatises*" ed. Wolfgang Leidhold, Indianapolis: Liberty Fund, 2004. Accessed December 2, 2011, http://oll.libertyfund.org/?option=com_staticxt&staticfile=show.php%3Ftitle=858&chapter=65974&layout=html#a_1607960.

Kloss, Jethro. *Back to Eden.* Loma Linda, CA: Back to Eden Publishing, 1992.

Manton, Thomas. "Mr. Thomas Manton's Epistle to the Reader." In *Westminster*

Confession of Faith, 9-12. Glasgow: Free Presbyterian Publishing, 1994.

Morecraft III, Joseph. *Authentic Christianity.* Powder Springs, Georgia: Minkoff Family Publishing & American Vision, 2009.

Myers, Kenneth A. *All God's Children and Blue Suede Shoes.* Wheaton, IL: Crossway Books, 1989.

Noah Webster's 1828 American Dictionary, 1828., s.v. "Agriculture." Accessed December 2, 2011, http://www.1828-dictionary.com/d/search/word,agriculture.

Rushdoony, Rousas John. *Systematic Theology.* 2 Vols., Vallecito, CA: Ross House Books, 1994

Russell M. D., Rex. *What the Bible Says about Healthy Living.* Grand Rapids, MI: Fleming H. Revell, 2006.

Weaver, Richard M. *Ideas Have Consequences.* Chicago and London: University of Chicago Press, 1984.

Webster's Revised Unabridged Dictionary 1913., s.v. "Beauty." Accessed December 2, 2011, http://1913.mshaffer.com/d/word/beauty.

Wines, E. C. *The Hebrew Republic.* Uxbridge, MA: American Presbyterian Press, 1980.

About the Author

Peter Bringe is a writer motivated to share the truth of God's word as it applies to our lives. In the area of food, this is a natural fit since he inherits an interest in food from his father, who is a food scientist. Around the dinner table, he has heard about the properties of various foods and the importance of food in health for as long as he's been eating. In addition to that, he has been interning with the Rocky Mountain Shepherd Center, taking classes from Whitefield College, and learning from his personal studies. Peter currently lives with his family in Elizabeth, Colorado, and enjoys various musical endeavors, writing, historical reenactments, and the study of many books.